Thoughts
about
God *and*
Life

DENNIS SULLIVAN

NEWMAN SPRINGS PUBLISHING
320 Broad Street
Red Bank, NJ 07701

First originally published by Newman
Springs Publishing 2024

All biblical citations were taken from
the New American Bible.

ISBN 979-8-89061-561-9 (Paperback)
ISBN 979-8-89061-562-6 (Digital)

Contents

Introduction

It's good to have answers. And sometimes, it's even better to have questions—the right questions. What should I do about that? What should I think about that? What other things should I think about? What do I believe?

Maybe this book will trigger some questions and other thoughts in you. Maybe some questions you will ask yourself or questions may just come to you, questions about life, questions about beliefs in God, and other thoughts.

This book is intended to present short reflections on a number of topics to give the reader some things to think about, one at a time mostly. Admittedly, it is offered to paraphrase the title of its predecessor book, to be merely one believer's thoughts—this believer. I hope that the thoughts are useful and the beliefs right, but that opinions are limited and discussable.

Saint Paul speaks of, "One God and Father of all, who is over all and through all and in all" (Ephesians 4:6). That means that the first five reflections on God really affect everything else in the book. And how each person believes (or does not believe) in God affects that person's whole life and every action.

I believe in God. If you don't, I invite you to join me in that belief. Of course, my faith is imperfect, and there is room for growth. If that more accurately describes you, then maybe you can join me in that effort to improve. The hope is that all of us can grow, move forward with the belief that a powerful, almighty, caring, Father-God is with us. His covenant with us is, "They shall be my people and I will be their God" (Ezekiel 14:11). And one of many other scripture references to the covenant says, "I will live with them and move among them, and I will be their God and they shall be my people" (2 Corinthians 6:16; Leviticus 26:12).

God—Knowing and Knowing About

This is about God. First a story. The preschool teacher said to four-year-old Billy, "Where does your father work?"

Billy said, "I don't know."

"Where did your father go to high school?" asked the teacher.

"I don't know."

"Do you know the year your father was born?"

"No, I don't."

So the teacher said to Billy, "Well, do you know who your father is?"

Billy said, "Sure. That's my father over there. Hi, Dad."

The point of the story, of course, is that there is a difference between *knowing about* and *knowing*. Little Billy didn't know everything about his father, but he *knew* him. Many people have some *knowledge about* God. They also even *know* God; and they can know him better.

I read that the Nicene Creed is officially accepted by the Catholic, Orthodox, and major Protestant Churches today. In addition to the Nicene Creed, the Apostles' Creed is popular, being officially accepted by Catholics and most Protestant denominations. The Nicene Creed basically grew out of Christian councils in the years 325, 381, and 451, when Christians were united. The Jewish Scriptures begin by talking about God.

A lot of people believe in God, not just my religious denomination and not just Christians.

That may be an interesting topic, but the focus here is on the first article of the creed that reads, "I believe in God, the Father Almighty, maker of heaven and earth, of all things visible and invisible."

Many believe that, and their Churches have for centuries. They say it at worship services, in one form or another, perhaps very quickly, and maybe not very thoughtfully. Catholics recite it. Even those who are saying the Rosary begin by saying the Apostles' Creed. I suspect most say it very quickly, not necessarily thoughtfully.

I believe in God, the Father Almighty, Maker of heaven and earth, of all things visible and invisible.

What believers know about God may be slightly different, but I assume that they believe in God, even know God, to some extent. God is the Creator of heaven and earth. Probably for centuries, that meant looking around at this flat earth and also looking up. Probably for us it also means the same thing. We believe in God, the Creator of this earth, this earth around us, everything that we see, and also means the sky, the dome over the top of us. I suspect that if we think about it, that is more or less what comes to mind when we say, "I believe in God the Creator."

Believers think about things, the big things that have been created, the oceans and mountains that we see. They think about the sun, the moon, the stars. And God created all of them. He created big things like those. He created little things, too, like pebbles, bushes, and grass, inanimate things.

But he also created small *living* things and big *living* things, animate objects—whales, sharks, elephants, cats, dogs, and birds. I read that, recently, a big whale breached the water and jumped onto a boat. God created big things like that, and he also created little things, really little things, like ants, tiny ants.

A few years ago, our family got a dog. My family has had dogs before, but this was somehow different. Because of this dog, I became much more conscious of living things—dogs, cats, squirrels, even ants, the birds we see everywhere. If a gecko gets into our house, I carry it out, if I can, rather than simply stepping on it or before the dog gets it and tries to eat it. I'll kill an ant if I see one in the house. I do it, but I also think about its being a living thing.

So what I am saying is that God is the Creator of all things, the Maker of all things, visible and invisible things, big things, little things, stars, planets, sun, moon, also rocks and grass and living things. Think about that. God is the Author of life. That's special.

And human things. That's really special. The human thing starts off as something really tiny, a couple of little cells, and then it grows, grows into something that can feel and then think and then decide and then love. And it is not just a human thing, a human "it." A human person is created.

"I believe in God, the Father Almighty, maker of heaven and earth, of all things visible and invisible."

And there's more.

God—Do We Think Big Enough?

Not long ago, I saw a photograph taken by a new NASA telescope. I think it's called the James Webb Space Telescope with which photographs can be taken of deep space. That raises this issue about God to a whole different level.

The NASA photograph shows new distances and sizes. It suggests greater times. The picture I saw looked like a picture of a mountain or something with substance, with a number of stars in the background. It turned out that this was a photograph of a huge area. When I say huge, I mean the caption spoke in terms of millions of miles, great distances. It spoke in terms of light-years. The distance between two points in this photograph was measured in light-years. I think it said many light-years.

I don't really understand all of that. I know what the words mean. I know what millions means, I know what miles means, I know what years means. I can give you the distance of a light-year, something like 5.88 trillion miles. But do I really "get" that? Do

I understand or appreciate what is a million light-years? I have to admit, I really don't fully comprehend that.

These NASA photographs raise the question of whether we need to expand our thinking. Do we have to expand our thinking geographically and temporally? Believers say, "I believe in God," God who created the earth and the heavens, and all things visible and invisible. With these photos, that means not just this earth that I see around me and this dome above us, but all of it, all that we see and is suggested in those NASA photographs. All of those millions of miles and light-years of space and eons of time; not just this earth and its sky, but all the heavens and this planet Earth, and the other planets and stars as well.

The universe is big in size and, of course, that is an understatement. Scientists also tell us that the universe has been around for a long, long time. They measure that not in years or centuries but in eons and light-years, numbers that surpass our understanding, at least mine.

It also raises the question of intelligence. This can't be an accident, can it? It couldn't have just been a coincidence, an explosion that just happened, and spread space things around, could it? How was it all started? Maybe there was an explosion at the beginning, but still, it had to be more, didn't it? Something or someone planned it, started it, and keeps it in existence. Something put order into it. Something guides it. Some intelligence, and an intelligence that is greater than anything I can comprehend.

The intelligence that we speak of is sufficient to create the size and space of the universe. But it also has sufficient ability to create living things as we have said before. It created large living things, like animals, and small living things, like insects and microscopic cells.

This intelligence also created living things that survived, grew, and reproduced.

This intelligence was also sufficient to create humans. In the first chapter of the book of Genesis, this creation of humans was first done merely by word and will, and later by taking part of one human being and creating a second one that was equal to the first. In either case, the book of Genesis is describing an all-powerful, intelligent God.

Theologians use words to describe God, like *all-powerful, infinite, all-knowing, intelligent, timeless, supreme being*. It is probably also correct to say that God is beyond all human understanding. And that believers are not thinking big enough and will always have to expand their thinking.

I call that power, that intelligence, God; the Israelites had a holy name for God. The rest of my belief will describe more about what that power, that intelligence, that God is like, what communication this God has had with all creation and with humans, what interaction, what caring.

But, as a start, I believe in God, the Father Almighty, Maker of heaven and earth.

God—I Know the One
Who Made This

I never met a president or a king. I think once, when I was young, on a school baseball field, I met a New York Knicks professional basketball player, throwing a baseball with a friend. I once heard President Bush (George W.) speak at an Annapolis graduation. I was at Yankee Stadium when a pope had a major event for tens of thousands of people. My wife once spoke with pro-golf legend Sam Snead. Msgr. David Toups (now bishop), who spoke with a group of us in the past, told us of a conversation he had with Mother Theresa. I shook Msgr. Toups' hand so I can now say, "I shook the hand that shook the hand of Mother Teresa."

But I really don't know famous people.,

But this thinking about God is different. God is a famous person (three persons, really, Father, Son, and Holy Spirit, in one God). God is important, more important than a president, more important than a sport figure, or even Mother Teresa. God is famous, is important, and he made all of this. All of this!

And I know him. I know this famous person. God made all of this, and I know him. In fact, he's my Father. It may sound flippant, but I know the guy who made all this, and he's my Father.

Is that being disrespectful? I don't think so. Saint Paul said to call God "Dad."

In his letter to the Romans (Romans 8:14–17), Paul says:

> For those who are led by the Spirit
> of God are children of God. For
> you did not receive a spirit of
> slavery to fall back into fear, but
> you received a spirit of adoption,
> through which we cry, "Abba,
> Father!" The Spirit itself bears
> witness with our spirit that we are
> children of God, and if children
> then heirs, heirs of God and joint
> heirs with Christ, if only we suf-
> fer with him so that we may also
> be glorified with Him.

And in Galatians (4:6–7), Saint Paul says, "As proof that you are children, God sent the Spirit of his son into our hearts, crying out, 'Abba, Father!' So you are no longer a slave but a child, and if a child then also in heir, through God."

Abba Father. I looked up in Google the word *Abba* and read that the word *Abba*, a Hebrew word, refers to the intimate relationship of father and child with the trust that a child puts in his daddy.

A pastor of mine one time said that the word *Abba* can be translated "Daddy, Dad, even Pops." Maybe Pops is pushing it, but okay.

Jesus basically said the same thing. He said, when you pray, say, "Our Father, hallowed be thy name." That's very formal language, a formal translation. Today, speaking with my earthly father, I would probably say it informally, "Dad, you're really special." Father, hallowed be your name, hallowed be you, Dad. Or on the golf course, I would say, "Dad, you're good. Nice shot."

When I see a NASA photograph of stars and planets, I could say something like, "Dad, that's really good, that's beautiful," although with others around, I would probably prefer to speak more formally, like a president's child might do at a public meeting.

But the point is that God is somebody really important, more than anyone, and I know him. I know God, and I am related to God.

Intellectually, I believe that, and I'd like to believe it even more deeply and I'd like to think about God knowingly and personally, the way I think about my earthly father, Jim.

God—Do We Think Near Enough?

There's another aspect of God, and that is how near God is to us and how approachable. Do we again have to adjust our thinking?

That NASA photograph speaks about light-years and distances, millions and billions, miles and light-years, centuries and eons of time. "A long time ago, in a galaxy far, far away," the movie said.

But the Old Testament and the Gospels remind us of God's proximity, his nearness. The Old Testament repeats, "I will be with you to help you" (for example, Isaiah 41:10; Jeremiah 7:23). I have made a covenant with you, a contract, an agreement. I will be your God and you will be my people (see for example Ezekiel 36:28; Genesis 17:7–8; Exodus 6:7). "I will be with you"; Emmanuel, which means God with us (Isaiah 7:14; see Matthew 1:23).

On the one hand, astronomy speaks about tremendous distances, light-years away, eons of time, billions of miles, millions of years. On the other hand, Scripture and faith speak about God with us.

Talk about extremes. It's almost a contradiction, but it's not. It's the extremes of God's greatness and his nearness.

God personally called Abraham (Genesis 12:1–3). He communicated with Moses, first in the burning bush (Exodus 3:1–3). He travelled with the Israelite people throughout their journey. They believed, especially in the Ark of the Covenant, that they brought with them that symbolized God's presence with them, and was to them more than just a symbol. They believed that God was really present with them.

They had this belief in God with them, and frequently, through their prophets, they repeated the words of the covenant, I will be your God and you will be my people. I will be with you to help you (see for example Isaiah 41:10).

And then there is Christmas. Again, the extremes of God. At Christmas, believers (and nonbelievers as well) sing the Christmas carol, "What Child Is This?" I was wondering about that. *Wait, why talk about a child, a little baby? I'm talking about God, an all-powerful God, Creator of the universe, eternal, timeless, limitless. Why are you talking about a baby? A helpless baby in a cradle, in a manger, in a stable? Poor.*

Why is Christmas about a baby? We're talking about the Almighty God who became Man.

But then I thought, isn't that the issue that the apostles brought up when they asked Jesus, "Are you now going to establish your kingdom?" (Acts 1:6); you know, take charge, use your power, the power of God, establish your kingdom, the kingdom of your Father.

Jesus had addressed that before (Matthew 20:25–28). He must have said something like, "You still don't get it. You're right. God is bigger than you realized and more intelligent and more powerful. God is really big. But it's not like that. He is powerful, yes, but he is loving and kind, and he is present with us, for us."

The Epistle to the Philippians 2:5–11 may have been an early Christian hymn, bringing together the extremes of God's majesty, power, and glory on the one hand and God's nearness, care, and understanding on the other.

In Philippians 2:5–8, we read that Jesus humbled himself:

> Who, though he was in the form
> of God, did not regard equal-
> ity with God something to be

grasped. Rather, he emptied himself, taking the form of a slave,
coming in human likeness; and
found human in appearance, he
humbled himself, becoming obedient to death, even to death on
a cross.

But verses 9–11 continue:

Because of this God greatly
exalted him, and bestowed on
him the name that is above every
name, that at the name of Jesus
every knee should bend, of those
in heaven and on earth and under
the earth, and every tongue confess that Jesus Christ is Lord, to
the glory of God the Father.

In Jesus, God became man—one of us—and
this is whom we worship. Yes, extremely majestic
and powerful, but yes, extremely close, caring, and
understanding. This passage brings together the
extremes in Jesus, man, and God—his lowliness and

his royalty, his emptiness and his resurrection, and his nearness yet the greatness of God.

In the temptations of Jesus (Matthew 4:1–11; Luke 4:1–12), the devil offered him all the kingdoms of the world, but Jesus, in effect, said, "No, it's not that kind of kingdom I'm establishing. It's not like an earthly kingdom. It's a kingdom based on faith in the Father and in me. It's based on love, kindness and forgiveness and justice. It is not going to be with palaces and strong armies."

He is telling us the kingdom is within us, maybe like what we see when people help each other, the kindnesses we see, the generosity.

And God is very approachable. Maybe that's why he came as a baby. Nothing is as approachable as a little baby. Everybody likes little babies and can approach them. "Isn't he (or she) cute?"

Does our thinking reflect all of that, his suffering and his risen life, the extremes of God in Jesus' nearness and his greatness, his humility and his majesty?

The extremes of God. He is royal yet he is also approachable.

God—And Us

When we think about God, there's a lot of "not only but also…"

God is not only the Creator of a really big universe, some of which is far away, but also he is very near to us. He was not only the Creator in the beginning but also is the one who continually holds everything in existence and guides it. He is not only the God of history of the Israelites centuries ago but also the God and guide of our history now and all history. Jesus, the Son of God, was not only a historical figure who lived two thousand years ago but also the Risen Lord who lives with us now.

How do we fit in with that? What does that have to do with us?

Christians believe they have different titles. They are the People of God, called by God in a special way and invited to him as all people are invited. They are the Body of Christ, united with Christ in a way that is compared to a human body (1 Corinthians 12:12–

27). One may be a foot, another a hand, others are eyes, but each is important, and each has a role.

Jesus said that he is the vine and his followers are the branches (John 15:1–8). My grandmother had a trellis in her backyard on which she had a grapevine. To me, the vine and the branches were so intertwined that one couldn't be sure where the vine ended and the branch began, but perhaps that is exactly the message that the Lord wishes to give with this comparison. We are that close to him and united to him that way.

Christians believe they are called in this way, not to be special or privileged but rather to be beneficiaries and servants, people who serve the Lord and are called to serve others and to invite others. But they believe they are united with God, at least imperfectly.

"Christians believe…" It's fine to say that, but the goal is for each individual also to be able to say, "I believe…" The goal is to say, "I also am a child of God the Father"; "I also am part of his people"; "I also am a member of the body of Christ"; "I also am a branch on the vine which is Christ." Christians believe they also are filled with the Spirit that was given to the Apostles on Pentecost and that the Spirit of God lives within them. Christians believe these things, and they try to get to the point where they say, "Not only do Christians believe" but "I also believe."

This is the God that is within us, the Triune God, the Father Creator, the Son Redeemer, and the Spirit of Pentecost. Of course, we are not perfect, we are not fully what we should be, but that's who we are in a limited and imperfect way.

And imperfect is okay because the message that Jesus brings is good news. I read somewhere that the good news (the meaning of the word *Gospel*) of Christianity means forgiveness and belonging. God forgives us, forgives imperfections. God calls us to be his children, even with our faults. Jesus brings that word *Abba* Father. We are forgiven, and we belong.

We know God, not just know about him. But we can always know him better and know more about him. But we are invited to share his life and already do so imperfectly. That is something to ponder. That is what we believe. "I believe in God the Father Almighty, maker of heaven and earth, of all things visible and invisible."

We give thanks, and we try to do better.

Why Didn't I Learn That Sooner?

Why didn't I learn that sooner? That sounds like the question of an older person, but actually, it could be asked to by anyone at any age. And it sounds a bit like, "Is it too late?" Well, it isn't, so let's get that worry out of the way.

Why couldn't I have learned it sooner, when I was younger or had more physical strength? I might have made different decisions. Things may have been different. If I had learned that sooner, I would have… If I had learned that sooner, I could have… I might have… I probably would not have done… But I definitely would not have done…

"Why?" is a tough question and usually not answered very clearly. Why does life happen that way? Why did things happen? Why does God let that happen? Why didn't I know then what I know now?

There may have been many reasons why that did not happen. Maybe I was too busy. I was trying to earn a living. I had a lot of issues.

Maybe I didn't try hard enough to learn. Maybe I was stubborn. Maybe I was just too young, maybe I did not have the opportunity, or nobody taught me.

Maybe I didn't listen hard enough or think enough. I didn't think about life. I didn't think about God. And maybe I didn't think enough about others.

Really, maybe it was just not my fault. And maybe I was just not ready to hear what God had to say to me. I did not have enough life experience then or enough wisdom.

There are some things, however, that we do learn. We learn that life is not a straight line. It's not perfect or perfectly clear. It's more like a journey, a long journey, that has many stops along the way. Some stops are really good. Some stops are bad, and maybe some are really bad; and maybe some just are. But the journey is not over till it's completely over.

The Old Testament people, early on, had a very long journey, some forty years before they reached their promised land (book of Exodus). And even then, that promised land was not the final goal, the final promised land as it turned out.

Jesus taught a lot. One of his major themes was forgiveness. That means that the people he was addressing had experienced mistakes, errors, sins. They needed forgiveness. Detours were part of their journey, even after they had already begun. Detours were part of that journey. Jesus did not hand out prizes. He handed out forgiveness.

His message was for people who had not learned sooner. It was good news for people who were not perfect. The prodigal son story was about a wayward son who was welcomed back home (Luke 15:13–32). The crippled man was told to pick up his mat and walk to prove that if Jesus could heal, he also had the power to forgive sins (Matthew 9:6). And there was the parable about some laborers who were hired only near the end of the day but were treated the same as those hired at the start of the day or at mid-day. They were all treated generously. They were all paid. The late hires were not penalized for arriving late (Matthew 20:1–16).

There are many things that one wishes he had learned earlier. In schools, he could've learned more. He could have observed more of other people, learned from them. He could have learned more from observing life and could have listened more to others, at work, from family, in life. Certainly, most people can listen more.

It is interesting to ask what I would do if I could do it over again, knowing what I know now. But it's more productive to ask what I should do now, knowing what I know now. A Franciscan pastor used to say, "Brothers and sisters, while we have time let us do good," a quote from Saint Francis of Assisi.

What would I tell or show someone else that I know now that I wish I knew then? What would I tell someone younger? What advice would I give? What example would I show?

I often return to Jesus' command, "Be perfect just as your heavenly Father is perfect" (Matthew 5:48), recognizing that I am not perfect, people are not perfect, the world around me is not perfect. I try continually (or maybe just often) to learn how to be better, if not yet perfect. I've heard it said, "It's never too late to do the right thing."

Saint Paul spoke about waiting for "a crown of righteousness" but only after reminding his followers that he had already competed well and had finished the race (2 Timothy 4:7).

And Jesus did not say, "It is finished" until it was actually finished, and only then did resurrection and complete new life happen.

But If It's from God

Is it? Jesus started something some two thousand years ago. And he comes out of a tradition that started a long time before that. Should this movement be believed?

Back in the first century AD (Anno Domini—meaning the year of the Lord, by the way), the followers of Jesus tried to spread his message and seemed to be building something. The establishment leaders at the time were fighting them, persecuting them, and trying to squelch whatever it was they were trying to get going. However, one of those leaders, Gamaliel, advised that Jesus' followers should be left alone. If what they were doing was from human origin, he said, it would fail. But if it was from God, it could not be stopped (cf. Acts 5:34–39). That was an interesting position and one that even today seems to have a good basis in the way things work.

Today, for example, we celebrate businesses that are around for twenty years or fifty years or maybe even a hundred years for what seems to be a long time. My country looks with pride on its existence for two and a half centuries. That's a long time, and it hopes for a long future. History looks at major empires and countries that rise and then fall but without lasting forever.

Jesus lived some 2,000 years ago, and his ancestors passed over from Egypt some 1,250 years before that. Abraham, Isaac, and Jacob lived half a millennium earlier still.

Is this faith "of human origin" or "is it from God?" There are so many reasons why this faith should not have survived. There were threats to its existence in Old Testament times by wars, invasions, and exiles, seeking to wipe out the Jewish people. The Roman Empire was strong in Jesus' time and allowed Jesus himself to be executed. And as mentioned, right after that, those who tried to stay with his movement and promote his message were hunted down, persecuted, and often killed. There have been persecutions throughout the ages. In addition to threats from outside enemies, there were weaknesses and divisions inside the Church. Although there were many holy and saintly people who followed the Christian way, there were also leaders throughout Christian history who were weak and failed leaders, even self-interested. There were and are heresies and divisions. Even today, there exist anti-religious and anti-Christian biases.

Gamaliel, a respected Pharisee, reminded the people of unsuccessful contemporary movements that were put down by the leaders of the establishment. He advised the other leaders, however, to act with caution and to let the disciples go free. He advised, "'For if this endeavor or this activity is of human origin, it will destroy itself. But if it comes from God, you will not be able to destroy them; you may even find yourselves fighting against God.' They were persuaded by him" (Acts 5:39).

The Apostles, after being flogged, did not stop teaching and proclaiming Jesus as the Messiah, and the Church grew.

Arguments are made for the proof of the existence of God, such as from creation (see Wisdom 13) or from philosophy or arguments from experiences of individuals considered to be holy persons or from some who have had a type of conversion.

I would like to highlight this argument. But if it comes from God, it will last.

Perfection——Yes and No

Jesus said, "Be perfect, as your Heavenly Father is perfect" (Matthew 5:48). But I'm really not and, probably, neither are you. So how should we deal with that?

On the one hand, Jesus calls. He said that the whole Law and the prophets is summed up in the commandment to love God with your whole heart and your whole mind, and that the second is like it, that you should love your neighbor as yourself (Matthew 22:36–40).

Saint Paul said love is the greatest gift, and he described it. "Love is patient, love is kind. It is not jealous. Love is not pompous...it does not rejoice over wrongdoing but rejoices in the truth. It bears all things, believes all things, hopes all things, endures all things. Love never fails" (1 Corinthians 12:31–13:13).

And there are the Ten Commandments that are even a foundation for much of civil law.

Jesus calls, and on the other hand, we respond. Do we perfectly follow these directives? No. We are not morally perfect. And we're not even physically perfect either as all get sick, all of us.

At our Catholic liturgy, the Mass, the priest at the beginning says, "Let us call to mind our sins." I always have some things to "call to mind," and I suspect I'm not alone. Popes and nuns frequently "go to confession"; I bet they rarely say, "I have no faults to report and for which I ask forgiveness." Ministers in other faiths also confess their sins and regularly ask for forgiveness. The leaders have faults, and so do the followers.

So how do we reconcile that? Christ says, "Be perfect."

And we have to respond, "We're not." So are we hypocrites? Is Jesus asking too much? And how many chances do we get? How many do-overs? What about that?

The short answer is that Jesus is not asking too much, but he is constantly calling us to more, to be better. And that's okay. He should. And we are to keep trying, even if we fall short all the time. And that's okay because we do keep trying. And yes, we keep getting more chances and always will. God is a forgiving God. Psalm 136 says, "The Lord is good, his *love* endures forever" (emphasis added). Another translation says his mercy endures forever.

Maybe we can keep looking forward and keep looking back, *looking forward* and trying to do what he asks. Trying to be better, be more, be closer to perfect. And also *looking back* and keep asking for forgiveness and for help to move, to move forward morally and also physically. And quit worrying about it so much.

I believe a theologian would agree with this: to keep trying to better ourselves and to keep being forgiven (if our intentions are good, and if we're not kidding ourselves). And that's okay also because Jesus makes up the difference where our actions and thoughts fall short of our good intentions and where our actions and thoughts fall short of perfection in our generally okay lives.

"Oh happy fault" sings our liturgy at the Easter Vigil. "Happy fault of Adam that brought such a redeemer." It would be good to feel more of that, that even our own faults and imperfections show that God is okay with us because even though we're not perfect, still, God is okay with us. That is a very comforting, even amazing concept.

It would be good to believe that and accept it more strongly.

In 1 Corinthians 1:27, Saint Paul says that God chooses the weak to confound the strong. We boast in the Lord, not in our own works, for God chooses to show that it is his strength that brings about the good result, even through imperfect people like us. God's wisdom and redemption overcome the foolishness and sin that we have.

Forgiveness is a major part of the Gospel, the good news.

Does that mean we should be happy about our own weaknesses, faults, and wrongs, even sins? No, but they are reminders of God's goodness that he is a loving father to us, in spite of all the imperfections we have and the imperfect things we have done.

Jesus preaches to be perfect, but he's okay with imperfect.

Things Are Not Perfect

Things are not perfect in the world either. That's why we have police, firefighters, EMTs, doctors, and nurses, and repair people.

And people are not perfect. They do wrong and always have. Adam and Eve ate the forbidden fruit. We think of an apple. People built the Tower of Babel in order to be like gods and to leave a legacy. Cain killed his brother. People say that this woman, this man, is the love of my life, but even in the best relationships, there are little disagreements, imperfections, even if she or he is "the best thing that ever happened to me" and a wonderful life partner. And other people can let us down. The point is that life now is not perfect. Even if life is going well, it's not perfect.

We say "that's life" and "that's the way it is." We are told we have to accept that fact and that reality. And we do. The life we live is incomplete. Nothing major there, that's just the way it is. *We are told to accept it or at least to accept that that's the way it is and try to make it better.* And that's a good thing.

What do we do about it? People do try to fix the world. They work, they make things, they fix, they clean, they repair. And people seek happiness. They work for a better life, they seek, they hope, they build. They do love each other and help each other. Most people seek a better life, a better world. They seek a better job, they seek friends, they seek health, they look for a new home. And that's good. That's the way to deal with an imperfect world.

They often use the word *paradise.* "This vacation spot is paradise." Their new community is a paradise. "I love this house"; "I love this apartment, this job"; "This car is the best." Of course, *they are not paradise, not really.*

The Old Testament prophets warned people about worshipping idols. Of course, we don't worship idols, we say. That's for the ancients. We're just seeking things. But it turns out that these are often things that fall short of the final goal or don't lead to it.

It's very easy for the things we seek to become idols. Goals are good, but goals are not everything and are good only if they lead to our ultimate goal. The goals, good as they may be, cannot be our god. The true

God and the real God-life has to go beyond the temporary goals.

I think of a sports tournament. Individuals and teams train, practice, work to qualify for the tournament. They celebrate qualifying for that tournament. They are really excited when they qualify for the event. Then they win the first round, and they celebrate, but there is another team that loses that first round. There is, then, a second round, and the winner celebrates and is in "paradise," but there is another team that this time feels defeated. What was paradise for them is no longer. And even the team that wins it all quickly realizes that that victory, too, is temporary. Its memory may last for a time, even a long time, but that still falls short of being paradise, true paradise. It may not have been an idol, but as it turned out, it wasn't the ultimate goal of true and permanent happiness.

So what should be the complete goal, complete true paradise?

The first lesson is that *life is a journey and true and complete paradise only comes at the end.*

Yes, *some of that paradise can begin now.* "Eternal life" does begin partially now, but it is not complete. "This is eternal life, that they know you, the only true God, and Jesus Christ whom you have sent"

(John 17:3). So eternal life does partially begin now to the extent that we know the only true God and the one whom he has sent, but the fullness of that life can only come later.

We can know and live that eternal life with its true values and goodness, right now, at least partially, to the extent that we live the God-life and God-values, but even so, it is not full, not complete yet. We can have treasure right now, *the right kind of treasure*. And that treasure is not necessarily a lot of toys, really good things, and the best stuff. Happiness can be now, but the right kind of happiness. "Love is patient, love is kind…" (see 1 Corinthians 13).

Complete happiness comes later.

Something Good May Come from It

Sometimes, things happen, unexpected things, maybe problem things, maybe even serious problem things, but better results can come from them.

I lost my reading glasses.

Puh-lease, one may say, that is not an event that causes major analysis and thought. Yes, it was a worry, a concern, and, yes, it was at least a nuisance. You do need your reading glasses to read longer items, but this is certainly not a life-changing circumstance or tragedy. I agree.

After some searching and efforts at solution, there was at least a short-term resolution of the problem. A temporary pair of reading glasses was purchased inexpensively at a local drugstore.

So what's the issue? What's the big deal? Did some significant "good" come from that? If so, what was it? What was the "something good" that could come of that?

Actually, nothing big did result. This time. It was only the thought, the thought that sometimes good things do come about from problems. For me, that was the only identifiable "good result." The thought. The idea, the idea that, sometimes, good things do come from problems. We've all heard that before, so this was just a reminder.

But it did make me think of more serious issues. I thought about the man on TV who sells pillows. I thought about how his life changed, how he went from being seriously addicted to drugs with its related problems, to founding a successful company and finding faith.

It made me think of another man in a television commercial who lost his firefighter brother in the tragedy of September 11, 2001, at the World Trade Center in New York City. He lost a brother, but he turned that tragedy around into founding a charity that helps other families who had lost a loved one in the line of service to others.

I think of accident victims with serious injuries who changed their lives around and had something good come from it, not what they had planned, but good things, nevertheless. I think of surprise pregnancies, even unwanted pregnancies that resulted in loved and lovable children.

I've heard stories of individuals who took a financial problem or personal problem and turned it around, maybe into starting a successful business, maybe into finding their faith.

It made me think that life is for the long run, our whole lives. And that life is leading to something beyond. There is wisdom in looking at life as a whole, looking at life in the long term, where we are going, what we are really here for, and what happens to us after this life is over. God is with us now. God has a plan for us, both for now and also for after.

It made me think of the man in Jerusalem, two thousand years ago, who was wrongly convicted of a crime and suffered a horrible death. But that man's life inspired people for centuries, even two thousand years later, to do good works in his name, remembering him; and the people who, to this day, do the good works in his name. And they do them, not only remembering him and following his lessons from long ago, but they also do the good works believing, trusting that he is with them now, really with them, that he is alive and sharing his life with them.

So, sometimes, good things do come from what seems bad, from problems, annoyances, tragedies. Sometimes, good things do come from them.

For this "problem" of mine about the glasses, it was only the thought, the idea. That was a "good" that came from it. Not a big deal but something; an idea, a thought, a faith-related thought. But it was something.

And by the way, four days later, I found the glasses in an airport lost-and-found department. I assume that someone I did not know did a good deed, found my glasses, and returned them to the right place, and a helpful gate agent helped me get there. And those, too, were "something good."

Saint Paul said, "We know that all things work for good for those who love God, who are called according to his purpose" (Romans 8:28). That may be hard to believe at times, but it is something to think about.

The God-life within Us

An Anglican priest said recently that when she speaks to her church congregation on a Sunday, she thinks also about the people who are not there. The woman is the rector of what sounds to be quite an active parish in Toronto.

The thought is a good one. She is concerned, not only about those who are in front of her in the church but also those the Church was not reaching, those that she wished to bring in. The thought is a good one, being concerned about those who should be there, who would benefit from being there.

The follow-up question is why. Why would she want others there? The answer is probably that God wants more. God wants to give us more, to increase the God-life in each of us; and He wants us to be more and to do more.

The word *God-life* reflects the Holy Spirit, grace. It reflects a belief in the Holy Spirit that is in people. It is the Spirit that the apostles received on Pentecost; it is the Spirit that Christians receive in their baptism and their baptism/confirmation. It is the life of God in each person. God wants people to have that life. He wants people to live that life. He wants that life to be more and to be deeper. And He wants that life to be lived more. The priest was most likely saying that she believes people will strengthen that life if they are present in the church and with that Church community.

God wants that life to bring greater peace, more happiness to the individual. That life is "good news." And then he wants that God-life to be lived more in the world. It is God's world, and the intent is to have that world be better, to be more of God's world.

It is really a cycle. We are to have that God-life within us for our own happiness and well-being, but we are also to have that "God life" in us to then bring into the world, to make the world more Godlike. It's good for people to be present.

But there are many that have the spark of this God-life in them but do not consider themselves part of the Church. They are not there in the church building. There are many such people. Their attitudes, values, life, and actions give evidence of that spark, but they may not even realize it. Being "in church" with the Church, with believers, can help them see what is in them already and name it. There are others who likewise have a small spark, and for them, also, it can be more, both for their benefit and the benefit of the world.

There's no question there are difficulties and problems in the world. Individuals' lives have problems for the individuals themselves, for their families, and for the world at large. And the world does have many divisions, many problems, and many moral issues.

The good news is that the God-life brings peace and joy for individuals. But there are also more difficult, more serious, harder issues, many problems, and many evils in the world. Believers need to be stronger, better prepared, better people to address those world problems and bring a God-life into it. Hopefully, being in the church with the Church community can help strengthen them. It is also good to think of those who are not in this building, this church building, with this Church community, and whose God-life hopefully can be strengthened to bring that God-life into God's world.

Those not there may include the leaders, business, government and political leaders, those especially in a position to make this a better world. But we have seen that sometimes God chooses the weak to confound the strong, the foolish to confound the wise (1 Corinthians 1:27–31). And so the call to increase God's life within us is a call for all, for the leaders but also for those who are not necessarily in positions of power. Those who are here may be the ordinary, the weak, the foolish. They can invite others, sure, but the call of God is to each person, to strengthen the God-life in themselves, to bring it to their world, even if their world seems particularly small. After all, our efforts help but when everything is said and done, it is God's power that makes it all work.

As Saint Paul said, we can plant and water, but God is the one who brings the increase (1 Corinthians 3:6–8).

It's Not What I Planned to Do

I had a plan for that day. It was nothing major, just a plan for the day, a schedule, a worthwhile project, something that I should do and wanted to do. We all do that. There are tasks that we have to do, work that is required. We sort things out, we decide what to do.

But then I heard, "Dad, can you help me with something?"

We have plans. Daily chores that are planned; there are budgets for home, for school, for work, or for business. Schedules and agendas. We have an overall plan. We have short-term plans. We have life plans, we have life goals, we have careers that are planned. Most plans are quite informal, but then something happens. Life interferes. Something that can't be avoided.

Some of the interruptions are small and easily handled. "Dad, can you help me with something?" Parents know that all too well, especially mothers with very young children, and dads, too, I should say, who would rather stay asleep than get up for a crying child. There are little things that interfere with our plans.

But there are big things that interfere as well. Life events, work events, financial issues. Mistakes. Decisions are made by others that affect us. Illness, and maybe much more serious than a common cold. Life changes or life causes change. Life interferes with our plans.

Or maybe it is correct to say that God interferes. God interferes with *our* plans, *my* plans.

An important part of faith is accepting the difference between our plans and what life sends our way; between knowing what we want to do and knowing what may be God's will for us and accepting the difference.

We pray, perhaps daily, "Our Father… Thy will be done." That's easy to say on a Sunday morning in church, in quiet time, by ourselves, on a retreat, on vacation. But in the middle of life, it's not easy to say. It's not easy to say when things do not go our way or as we had planned. What does the parent do when the baby cries in the middle of the night? A good night's sleep had been planned. A healthy child had been hoped for or a spouse who would live forever, healthy.

A teenage girl heard an angel tell her that she was to conceive and bear a son, and she would name him Jesus. In Saint Luke's Gospel (Luke 1:46–55), Mary's prayer sounds calm, "My soul proclaims the greatness of the Lord; my spirit rejoices in God my Savior." This prayer sounds very peaceful and confident, but I wonder whether she was terrified by the message because it probably did not match the plans that she had for herself. In fact, the reading says she was troubled by this, and the angel had to tell her not to be afraid. But because of her acceptance of life's interference with her plans, the world would change. "May it be done to me according to your word," she said (Luke 1:38).

Years later, at a wedding, this same mother said to her Son, "They have no wine." The Son indicated that it wasn't in his plans to do anything about that at that time. But he answered her unspoken request, and with the miracle of changing water to wine, Jesus began his public ministry (John 2:1–11).

We live our faith, not in a vacuum but in the midst of real life. We have our plans, plans that seem good, but life interferes or maybe it is God who interferes, and we are called to live that faith in the real world.

Jesus was born into the real world, not into some make-believe situation. Planning is important; it's good for us to make *our* plans, but God has *his* plan in this real world. The believer's task is to say, "May thy will be done." The believer's task is to accept life's interferences and to deal with them. In football, they refer to that as an audible, where a quarterback or other player chooses a different plan based upon what he sees in the world he faces.

The believer, the faith person, does his best planning, yes, but making changes when required and accepting those changes when life interferes and when God interferes. It is *God's* will that is to be done, *his* plan that is to be accepted.

There can be real interior peace in accepting life's interference or God's interference, even when that interference smashes one's plans. After all, he's the Father, the Dad, and he does not mind helping.

Moses Broke the Tablets

Moses broke the stone tablets, not the Ten Commandments themselves, of course. He broke the stones that he had brought down from the mountain (Exodus 32:19). He was that angry. Is there a lesson here for us?

The Lord had been good to the people. He had freed them from slavery in Egypt and brought them out into the desert. They had miraculously gone through the waters of the Red Sea, and their pursuers were defeated. They were now on their way to the promised land with a new freedom because of God's help. Can't we identify with some of that? Haven't we also been fortunate?

Instead of being grateful for good things that they had received, however, they were impatient, waiting for Moses to come down from the mountain. They failed to recognize from where their good fortune had come, from whom it had come. They had turned to other gods. In fact, they had melted their gold and fashioned gods of their own. They then worshipped those fake gods in ways that they thought those gods would appreciate. Moses was understandably angry and smashed the stone tablets on which were written the Commandments that had been given to him and to them, the Commandments which were "inscribed by God's finger" (Deuteronomy 9:10).

This whole event involved the establishment of a covenant, a two-party contract. As God said, the contract was "You shall be my people, and I will be your God" (Ezekiel 34:28, see also Exodus 6:7 and Genesis 17:8–9). Both parties assumed obligations. For his part, God assumed the obligation that "I will be with you to help you." The other party to the contract was the people, and they, too, had an obligation—"and you will be my people." That meant that the people could rely on God but also that they were to live according to God's values and his requirements and his laws.

Those values and laws were written in stone and signed, not on a paper contract or in a written constitution, but with a covenant sacrifice, the way it was done back then. God had promised help and protection, and they in turn were to show loyalty and fidelity to him and show proper behavior by their actions. "You shall carefully observe the commandments, the statutes, and the ordinances which I enjoin on you today" (Deuteronomy 7:11).

But the people had rejected that arrangement, and instead followed gods that they themselves had made out of gold.

What's the lesson for us? Haven't we today also received gifts? Haven't we received freedom and promises for the future in our personal lives and in our countries? And how have we responded? Have we been loyal, grateful, and trusting in God's help? Or have we grown inpatient and made other gods and worshipped those gods? Have we carefully observed "the Commandments, the statutes, and the ordinances that I enjoin on you today"?

News stories in the media and elsewhere would suggest some of each: some faithfulness, some not. There is goodness shown in good news stories—selflessness, generosity, caring; we also hear of wrongdoing, self-centeredness, injustice, and harm. In a single, typical newspaper or news report, we can learn of violence, divisions, war, theft, infidelity, prejudice, and dishonesty, even blasphemy. One can almost hear Moses smashing the stone tablets.

And how does God, on his part, respond? Back then, in about 1250 BC, how did God respond?

God did not abandon his people. He did not walk away from them, rather he directed Moses to make new tablets like the first. In making those new stone tablets with the Commandments, in effect, he was giving his people another chance. He kept the covenant language. He showed himself to be a God who is merciful and forgiving (Deuteronomy 31:18 and following). He would be there to help, but they were to trust and be loyal to him and live properly. It would be a two-way street. As directed, Moses repeated God's promises that God would be with them to help them. But Moses also repeated the people's obligation that they were to be his people.

God said that he would be there but he would also not hold the guilty guiltless, whatever that meant. But there is no doubt that he stayed with his people, remained faithful to the covenant. On his part, he continued to lead the people toward and into the promised land. For their part, God wanted the people to be faithful. "I am the Lord your God who brought you forth from the land of Egypt. You shall not have strange gods before me." And he wanted proper behavior, proper values, a good moral code. "You shall not kill...steal...covet...bear false witness." Honor your parents, worship God (Exodus 20:1–17). Jesus fulfilled that in a new way using words like justice and love.

The Lord is a forgiving God, slow to wrath, merciful, and forgiving, but I will not hold the guilty guiltless (see Proverbs 11:21). Jesus did not describe that as a threat but rather that the covenant was a two-way street. In Saint John's first epistle, we are told, "If God has so loved us, so we also must love one another" (1 John 4:11).

The Exodus and Deuteronomy writings were written for that Hebrew community three thousand years ago. They are also written for us now, for our countries now, for our communities now, for our families now, for ourselves now. The covenant is still a two-way contract that God promises to be with us to help us now, and we promise to be his people living according to his values now.

If we fail to carry out our part of the contract, Moses is not here to get angry and to smash the stones, but his message remains. God won't abandon us and will continue to be merciful and forgiving, but we are not to take that for granted. As we have been loved, so must we love one another (see John 13:34). The arrangement is still the covenant-contract, a two-way street, a two-party arrangement.

God gives forgiveness easily, but it helps to accept the obligation and want the forgiveness.

But Those Are Moral Issues

The radio had a news report about proposed abortion legislation. The report summarized the proposal, then had the sound bite of a woman who opposed the legislation. She argued, "Abortion is about healthcare, and they want to make it a moral issue."

But isn't it a moral issue? Isn't it a question of right and wrong? Isn't that what people usually mean by calling something a moral issue?

Many, if not most, issues in our lives have to do with that question: is it right? Or is it wrong? Is it good or not good? And many people would argue that society would be better off if that question were top of mind for a lot of people.

The woman's comment reminds me of the mobster in a *Godfather* movie, who says to the man he is about to kill, "It's just business. It's just business, not personal," he said, expecting his victim to understand. But one can and should ask about the morality of an action, even though it is just business or because it is "just a medical procedure."

Many things in life are moral issues, that is, issues as to whether an action is right or wrong. *What is right, what is wrong, what's ethical?* One may be just short of money, but taking money from another is still a moral issue, that is, is it an honest transaction? Or is it stealing? Is shoplifting stealing, wrongfully taking from another and, therefore, wrong? Or is it somehow justified? Some questions need to be asked and asked by many.

One may be "just lonely," but fidelity is still a moral issue. That is, is this an appropriate friendship or is it infidelity to another person or obligation? One may not like a government or business policy and have a legal right to protest, but does one's right to protest violate another person's rights? Damaging property is still a moral issue. Is the method of protest right or is it wrong? As well as is it legal or not legal? Does it violate another person's rights? People may disagree politically, but the way of objecting is still a moral issue.

Immigration laws should reflect a balance of protecting the rights of current citizens and fairly caring for others and sharing justly the world's goods and opportunities. Enacting just laws is a moral decision. That is, are they right or are they wrong and are they fair? The way those laws are enforced is also a moral issue. Is it right or is it wrong? And what about a public official who takes an oath before God to enforce laws?

A government official is entrusted with other people's money paid in taxes. Is proposed legislation or action justified in spending people's money? That's not an easy issue, but it is an issue nonetheless.

Society has laws that should be good laws, and that form the basis of a good society. Religion has laws and rules, such as the Ten Commandments or the two great commandments that Jesus refers to summarizing the whole Law and the prophets, namely to love God above all things and to love one's neighbor as oneself. Those major laws are enacted for a reason and for a better society. They are supposed to be positive moral issues that prescribe what is right and what is wrong.

"They are trying to make this a moral issue." Well, very likely it is a moral issue and should be. Many things are. Intelligent people are to consider the morality of issues. And laws. God-believers should consider the morality of issues and act rightly, loving God above all things and loving neighbors as themselves.

And there are many more issues that are moral issues and require thought and review. Many religions encourage their members to take time to examine their lives, to examine their consciences, to evaluate whether they are living according to the principles by which they should be living. Many Christians use the time of Lent and preparation for Easter as a time for an examination of conscience, self-examination. Jews use Yom Kippur, the day of atonement, to examine their lives.

All people can look at themselves and examine their actions and thoughts, examine their consciences. They can look at their obligations to themselves, to others near to them, to God, to others in the world, and to the world itself. These reflect moral issues.

I, we, God, others, world

I—have I acted to take care of and improve myself, my health, knowledge, work, education, and to live up to my potential?

We—how have I fulfilled my obligations to those close to me, my family, my spouse, parents, and children?

God—how have I fulfilled my obligations to God, to be fully the child of the Father that I am called to be? Have I prayed often, have I prepared for worship and actively participated in it?

Others—how have I fulfilled my obligations to others, my friends, and to those in need? Have I worked as I should, treated others justly, fulfilled the obligations of my oaths, my contracts, my promises?

World—how have I fulfilled my obligations to protect the world, its air, water, and living things? To act to end injustice, racial prejudice, poverty, and hunger?

A periodic examination of conscience is a good thing, and it's good to be followed by a prayer for forgiveness and of trust that forgiveness is forthcoming from a fatherly, loving God.

Life is filled with moral issues. Is this right? Is it wrong? What should I do? What am I called to do?

Moral issues.

Miracle or Coincidence

A friend of my wife met Pope John Paul II face-to-face. The story is interesting.

The friend's husband had been a well-respected heart specialist. Years ago, he was called in to treat a priest who had a serious heart issue. The doctor took care of the priest and treated him, but the problem was very serious.

Six months or a year later, he met with the priest. To his surprise, the priest was healthy. He had recovered from the heart problem. The doctor, however, saw no medical reason why his condition should have improved so much that the man was back to health.

He asked the priest what he did, but the priest responded that he had done nothing special. He had resumed his normal life. He had not changed any daily routine.

However, he did pray to Faustina Kowalska, who later became known as Saint Faustina.

Faustina was a Polish religious nun who died in 1938, at age thirty-three. Apparently, she was thought by many to be a special, prayerful woman, considered to be very holy. Faustina had a very deep devotion to the divine mercy of Jesus, the kindness of Jesus, and his forgiveness. She was well-known for that devotion and promoted that blessing of Jesus.

There developed an effort to have her declared a saint. A process in the Church had begun for her canonization, and evidence of something possibly miraculous was considered.

The doctor who had treated the priest was a good man but not especially religious and certainly not an enthusiast of miracles. He was asked to give testimony in the canonization process of Faustina about the events with his priest-patient. Apparently, he testified as to how he treated the priest and about the priest's recovery. He further testified that he knew of no medical reason for the man's return to health. And he reported about the priest praying to Faustina.

On April 30, 2000, Faustina was declared a saint by Pope John Paul II, later known as *Saint* Pope John Paul II.

After the canonization ceremony, there was a luncheon in the Pope's private dining room with about fifty dignitaries and various celebrities. It was also attended by the doctor and his wife. She said that there she met the Pope. He held her hand and looked her straight in the eyes. It was a warm, powerful feeling. She felt as if he could see right into her, right through her. For her, it was a special moment, one she wouldn't forget.

On the day of Faustina's canonization, John Paul II designated the first Sunday after Easter, that Sunday as "Divine Mercy Sunday." On that day, the Gospel reading describes Jesus showing mercy and kindness to his apostles, those who had not stood by him during his crucifixion and death. He treated them with great kindness, especially Peter who had denied him while his judicial process was ongoing before Pontius Pilate and the other officials.

On April 22, 2001, which was one year after establishing that first Divine Mercy Sunday, Pope John Paul II reemphasized its message in the resurrection context of Easter. He said, "Jesus said to St. Faustina one day: 'Humanity will never find peace until it turns with trust to divine mercy.'" Divine mercy! This is the Easter gift that the Church receives from the Risen Christ and offers to humanity.

Faustina is considered the Apostle of Divine Mercy. Pope John Paul II, Saint Pope John Paul II, died on April 2, 2005, which was Divine Mercy

Sunday. He was later canonized a saint on Divine Mercy Sunday, 2014. The woman's husband, the doctor, died on Divine Mercy Sunday, 2010.

Coincidence?

God acts in funny ways sometimes.

Divisions, Differences, Rivalries, Biases

Divisions, differences, rivalries, and biases. They are all separations, but they do not all have the same effect. Believers can ask, "Where do I fit? Is my vision clear or clouded? Am I a uniter or a divider?"

There are many *divisions* in the world. There is political Left and Right, Liberal and Conservative, Democrat and Republican. Surprisingly strong divisions. Historically, there was Athens and Sparta, Rome and Greece, Jewish and Gentile, Old World and New World. There have been Christians and Muslims. Today, there is Israel and Iran, abortion and antiabortion, coastal cities and rural towns, divorced husband and divorced wife.

Taken to the extreme, these *divisions* hurt everyone. The parties are separate, may not communicate, not work well together, not share their strengths; they may fight and even war against each other.

There are also just plain *differences*. People have different ethnic backgrounds, different histories. There are different opinions. Such differences can be good. People can listen and learn.

Parties learn from each other, enjoy the benefits of each other's cultures, learn from each other's histories, backgrounds, and strengths. Food is an example. There is Mexican, Chinese, Italian, French, fried, and barbecued. We share and enjoy foods and even have buffets with foods from many nations and backgrounds.

And people intermarry. At a college event a number of years ago, parents of new freshmen met for a parents' night at the beginning of the school year. At one table were four young freshmen, each with an Irish last name. They learned at dinner that the mother of each of them had a Polish maiden name and Polish ancestry. These young Irish-Polish Americans became friends, learned together, and found that they shared values and religion, probably of their ancestors. The common religion was not a surprise since it was a Catholic college.

There are *rivalries* in sports in particular: Florida-Georgia (college football), Army-Navy, Texas-Oklahoma, Alabama-Auburn, Notre Dame-USC, Ohio State-Michigan; Green Bay-Chicago in professional football; Yankees and Red Sox in baseball. *Rivalries* are certainly fine, and while there is strong competition, there often results a great respect for the opponent. The loser hates to lose, but if the game is played properly, the losing team may congratulate the winner, and a well-played competition can lead to mutual respect. Yankees fans cheered a Red Sox slugger when he retired, and Red Sox fans cheered a great Yankee pitcher when he did the same. Of course, there had been no such appreciation and love when the player had been active and caused difficulties for the respective hometown team. But respect grew, and appreciation was shown.

Biases. It's hard to see how bias is a good thing. Bias usually means that one party assumes itself better than the other. It sees little value in interaction and intercommunication with members of the other party. Any benefit from interaction is absent.

There are most likely other categories and sub-categories, but that's the idea.

The question for each individual should be "Where do I fit?"; "What are my disagreements, different opinions, preferences, personal feelings?"; "Are they irreconcilable *divisions*?"; "Are they *biases* that cloud and blind vision?"; "Are they only *differences* of background, history, or opinions that can be communicated and discussed?"; "Are they merely good-fun *rivalries*?"

Those are good questions for self-reflection. Where am I? What are my relationships, my separations? Are they irreconcilable divisions, differences, rivalries, biases? How can I better hear and speak? That is, how can I improve my own communication, listening as well as speaking?

Some commentators call the book of Jonah the high point of Old Testament theology. They say that because in the book of Jonah, God is presented as the God of all, not only the God of one people.

Jews and Samaritans, at the time of Jesus, did not get along, they did not associate. Yet Jesus spoke with the Samaritan woman at the well in John 4:4–30. Jesus engaged her in conversation, and she became one who told others about Jesus and asked whether He could be the Messiah.

Jesus also spoke a parable about a Good Samaritan (Luke 10:29–37), emphasizing that there is goodness in all people, even in one's competitors and enemies.

Saint Paul pushed Christianity out from the Jewish-only community to one that included Gentiles, all peoples.

One can ask, "How do I think about others? How do I treat them? How do I listen?" One can ask, "How does God think about them?"

Why Is There Suffering?

Why is there suffering? Why do bad things happen?

First of all, like many others, I don't know. I just don't know. But as I have said many times in the past, I believe there is a reason. I just don't know what it is. I can tell you, however, what I see; maybe that can help.

Sometimes, I see good things come about from bad things. While his wife was in the hospital and recovering, each day for two weeks, the husband was brought dinner by a different neighbor. A man sitting in the waiting room in the doctor's office didn't realize that his leg was bleeding. It was just a small spot, and a lady nearby pointed it out and gave him a tissue. There was a car accident and strangers stopped to offer assistance. Someone fell, and the same thing happened.

There was a hurricane, and people came to help. A family member had an unexpected but very serious medical emergency, and his sisters and brother traveled to be with him and show their support.

Is that why the bad things happened? Were these reasons, if not *the* reason? We don't know, but it's interesting how good people show goodness when someone else has a problem or gets hurt or faces a problem or has a need.

It makes one wonder. When people see a need, someone else's need, they step up to help. They are good people, to be sure, but it's then that they show special care. They release the God-life that is within them. They release that spirit of love, God's Spirit that is in each person. It's not that the God-life in them was not acted on before, but it seems that at times like these, they let it show more, maybe have it grow, and maybe become a better person through this action.

People are good, and, at times of need, they really show up.

It seems, however, that not all people are good. But maybe the needs of others can bring them around. Movies sometimes use that theme, end-of-life conversions, remorse, repentance, a good action, just before death. And there is the Good Thief on Calvary who showed goodness and caring for Jesus as the thief considered his own punishment to be just. One hopes for that, for conversion, goodness, even at the end. Maybe need and suffering, even suffering by another can lead to that.

Why did Jesus go through his suffering and death? Maybe some of the same thing, that suffering was necessary to bring out greater love and care in others. Maybe what he did motivated greater love, goodness, and effort in those who followed him, and has done so for a long, long time, centuries.

It seems that suffering is sometimes necessary as a part of the plan for conversion. The story of the Old Testament people is a story of relationship with God, followed by doubt and infidelity, followed by suffering, and then followed by redemption. Jacob's family in Genesis and Exodus had to migrate to Egypt. They became enslaved and only then returned to the promised land. Centuries later, in Palestine, the Israelites were overrun, then exiled to Babylon, and only after forty years were returned to their homeland.

Jesus suffered and was wrongly executed before rising to new life. Christians throughout the ages have been martyred only to strengthen the Church. Tertullian, an early Christian author said, "The blood of martyrs is the seed of the Church." And maybe our problems, small and large, somehow are the seeds of goodness, kindness, and a better life, sometimes in this life, but always after it.

"Thy will be done. Thy kingdom come." I guess there is a reason, even if we don't know what it is.

Yeast and Salt

I don't make bread, but the recipe I read calls for yeast, not a lot, to make the bread rise. I put salt on my food. It can give a better taste. And I turn on lights.

These are optimistic examples for our role in dealing with problems, family problems, community problems, world problems. A little yeast affects the whole loaf of bread. A little salt improves flavor. Light helps us see.

Jesus went up the mountain, the way Moses did, to give direction to his followers. He used the example of salt; he used the example of light, little things that can make a difference. He said, "You are the salt of the earth. You are the light of the world" (Matthew 5:13–16).

In Matthew 13:33, he used the example of yeast and said, "The kingdom of heaven is like yeast that a woman took and mixed with three measures of wheat flour until the whole batch was leavened." He also used the example of a mustard seed and referred to

"The smallest of all the seeds" (Matthew 13:31–32). Small things can make a difference. A small number of people can make a difference, just like the remnant that remained in the Old Testament after the exile (see e.g., Zephaniah 2:7–10).

He gave these instructions to all his followers—the group, the whole Church. But they also apply to each individual. So, on Sunday, when we hear about yeast and salt and light, we can think about ourselves. When Jesus says, "You are…salt, yeast, light," I usually hear that as "you" plural, that is all of us, and that's true. "You all," "all of you," "you-uns," "you guys," "*ustedes*," you plural. He is speaking to all his followers, his Church.

But shouldn't I also hear, "you," singular? "Hey, you," "hey, brother," "hey, sister," "*tu*"; you, singular? "You, yourself, individually, are to be salt for the earth"; "you yourself can be yeast"; "you yourself can be a light for others."

The one preaching necessarily speaks to all of us, the crowd, the congregation. But the message is also more targeted than that. It also can be for me, individually, not only for all of us together. I can hear it that way, I can hear a directive for me alone as well as for me with others.

In John 14:21, Jesus says, "Whoever has my commandments and observes them is the one who loves me." A friend who is not formally Judeo-Christian seems to have the Commandments and live what I call Christian values as do many other supposedly non-Christians who do the same. Their actions and lives demonstrate that. Another friend who claims "not to be religious" seems also to do similar things. He lives the values and does the actions that are those directed by the Lord. To repeat, Jesus said, "Whoever has my commandments and follows them is the one who loves me." Does that mean that people who act like that, do his will, and follow his commandments, "are the ones who love me?" Even if they think they don't know him?

I'm just asking.

In a book, *Salt of the Earth*, a journalist, Peter Seewald, interviewed Cardinal Joseph Ratzinger who became Pope Benedict XVI. In his introduction, Mr. Seewald says, "At one point I asked him how many ways to God there were. I really didn't know what he would answer. He could have said, 'only one' or 'several.' The cardinal didn't take long to answer: 'As many,' he said, 'as there are people.'"

That can cause a lot of thought.

The author later added the theological remarks by the cardinal about salvation who seems to recognize that the Lord is not limited by a person's conscious belief or unbelief in him. He seems to suggest that the way of the Lord is not so limited.

Here's the more complete question and answer:

Interviewer: How many ways are there to God?

Cardinal's response was that there are as many as there are people. For even within the same faith, each man's way is an entirely personal one. We have Christ's word: "I am the way." In that respect, there is ultimately one way, everyone who is on the way to God is therefore in some sense also on the way of Jesus Christ. But this does not mean that all ways are identical in terms of consciousness and will, but, on the contrary, the one way is so big that it becomes a personal way for each man.

The one way is so big that it becomes a personal way for each person. Isn't that a challenge? And for each of us? And doesn't that sound consistent with our experience that each person is both called and challenged?

Scripture seems to reinforce that "If we love one another, God remains in us, and his love is brought to perfection in us" (1 John 4:12). And "God is love, and whoever remains in love remains in God and God in him." (1 John 4:16).

Maybe there is a lot more yeast, salt, and light than we sometimes think.

I Felt Called

We've heard people say, "I felt called."

Often the word *vocation* is used to refer to something religious such as a person's desire to be a priest, a nun, a friar, a pastor, a missionary. Then, again, the word *vocation* can be broader than that and refer to what someone wants to do with his or her life, such as being a doctor, a lawyer, a public servant, in the military. It can refer to a field of study or a technical skill, such as nurse, electrician, plumber, carpenter, beautician; a parent.

A person feels a calling. Hopefully, it is a desire or a choice to do something with their lives consistent with good values, with God's will—a service or vocation to others and the world.

And so it happens. The person works toward this calling for a period of time, maybe a period of study and preparation, then maybe for a short time, maybe for a long time, of actually performing the desired service.

But then, sometimes, events happen, life happens, things change in one's life. It is said that "God writes straight with crooked lines." Something happens. A teen sustains a broken arm and so can no longer play on a baseball team, and that affects a possible future school career or sports career. Maybe a field of study does not work out. Or a job is lost through no fault of one's own or even because of one's own fault. Maybe there's an accident or an injury. Maybe pregnancy affects possible plans. Maybe there is an illness, physical or mental, to one's self or to a spouse, and that interferes with one's desired plans. Maybe a person makes a mistake. Maybe someone does something wrong.

Perhaps a person simply says he or she no longer wants to do this or can't. "This is no longer right for me" or "I feel called to something else." Or simply retirement. Or maybe the desired vocation never gets a chance to start.

What about vocation? Does that mean that one's original vocation no longer applies? It may, but does that mean that there is no longer a calling? Does it mean that the person no longer has a vocation?

Wouldn't it be more appropriate to use the word *vocation* to apply to a "calling" to anyone, at any age, in any circumstance? In fact, to everyone and now?

It certainly seems more appropriate to see vocation in that way. That way seems more consistent with a fatherly God who loves each and every person as they are, where they are. It seems more appropriate to believe in a calling from a Father who easily forgives, if that's what's needed, to see a calling with enough healing, if that's what's needed or with enough strength, if that's what needed to do the work of God. There have to be ways for each person to receive a call from God to honor that God and to care for others as God commands.

God frequently chooses the weak and has done so for centuries. Can't it be true that each person's calling, each person's vocation is to use his or her talents to help others, to care for others, to show love and caring, to show faith in some way now? Can't one make the world better in a career or job different from the original one or the desired one or in one's retirement or in a nonjob? Can't the good news and love be demonstrated by one who is out of work, is struggling, or ill, or disabled, or injured? Can't that be a vocation of which one can be proud?

Isn't it true that each person has a vocation now? The only question is, "What is it?"

What Catholics Can Learn

What Catholics can learn from other Christians.

This reflection is mainly for Catholics, but others can certainly listen in. It has some generalizations which one should avoid, so maybe a better title would be, "What This One Catholic Has Learned from Other Christians."

I am a lifelong Catholic and happy to be one and proud of it and expect to be Catholic for the rest of my life. I've studied a lot, probably more than most: schools, postgraduate theology, personal reading. There is a lot of good theology in this Church, and theologians, and a breadth of topics. There has been "high church" worship in cathedrals and stadiums, small group worship in homes and in hidden places during troubles. There is the Catechism of the Catholic Church, which presents a broad range of topics with very good theology. There is a large volume of documents from the Second Vatican Council. We have a rich liturgy and a full liturgical calendar that reflects our beliefs. There are many holy people now as in the past, doing heroic works. I am proud of that.

Sure, there are the weak and sinners. But, of course, we are all sinners. And there are other graces from the Sacraments, especially the Eucharist.

What's the point?

I participate in a men's fellowship in my community with men from many denominations, and there I've learned a lot. Most of our speakers are dedicated Christians, many of them ministers. What I have learned is the strong faith of many of my fellow Christians from other denominations. I've learned that their faith reflects a deep personal relationship and commitment to the Lord Jesus. It's personal and it's deep. These Christians have a deep belief in and appreciation of the Word of God in Scripture. They live their faith. That faith is outgoing; many are less hesitant about proclaiming their faith, showing and discussing it. In the Scriptures, Jesus says, "I am the way and the truth and the life" (John 14:6). Many Christians proclaim that unabashedly.

This is normally the part where one says, "But." There is no "but" here. There is only an "and." I believe in my Church, my Faith, *and* I have learned from my fellow Christians. Sure, there are many Catholics who have all of these characteristics, but I am impressed by the faith I see in these other Christian believers. I have drawn no deep conclusion from this other than to recognize that what I have learned has added to my faith and my beliefs. It's more like an underline of some of my beliefs. It's a highlighting of what I believe. I see the faith of my fellow Christians, their faith in Jesus, their faith in the Word of God, and their living of their faith. I am motivated by it.

What is my conclusion? I admire that, I appreciate that, and it adds to my faith. It's more an underlining, an emphasis. I hope other Christians can say the same about me.

Jesus prays, "I pray… So that they all may be one, as you, Father, are in me and I in you, that they also may be in us, that the world may believe that you sent me" (John 17:21). We pray that, someday, we may be one.

That points to the ecumenical movement where members of Christian denominations talk, pray, and act together with the hope of again becoming one, to fulfill that prayer of being one.

That effort continues and with the emphasis on the faith and works that we have in common, "One Lord, one faith, one baptism, one God and Father of all, who is over all and through all and in all" (Ephesians 4:5–6).

How Should I Think about Jesus?

How should I think about Christ, Jesus of Nazareth, Jesus the Messiah, Jesus the Christ? I don't just mean intellectually and theologically, like someone you read about. I mean personally, the way you think about a friend, a relative, a spouse, a child.

I consider myself as religious, a person of faith. I think about God, the Lord. I say, "O God" or "Lord" when praying. And I do pray. I try to do good, do what's right. I go to church. I try to live a good life, fulfill my responsibilities. But how should I think about Him—Jesus the Christ?

A selection from Saint Paul's letter to the Ephesians (Ephesians 1:3–12) is read on the Feast of the Immaculate Conception, December 8:

> Blessed be the God and Father of
> our Lord Jesus Christ, who has
> blessed us in Christ with every

spiritual blessing in the heavens, as he chose us in him, before the foundation of the world, to be holy and without blemish before him. In love he destined us for adoption to himself through Jesus Christ…

In him we have redemption by his blood, the forgiveness of transgressions…he has made known to us the mystery of his will…

In him we were also chosen…

Notice some keywords or phrases in that reading:

- Blessed us in Christ
- Chosen
- To be holy
- Adoption
- Forgiveness
- Has made known to us

In that letter, Saint Paul says that God, the Father, has *blessed* us with every spiritual blessing in the heavens. I have been blessed. I am grateful for that. My life has been good, and I understand a lot about what I have and how I have been blessed. And I trust about what I don't understand.

But Paul says that I have been blessed *in Christ.* That is, not alone but in Christ. (Paul says) God, the Father, has *chosen* us *in him.* Again, not alone and not by myself or ourselves but *in Him.*

Think about that. That's pretty deep. I am chosen in Christ.

He adds that we were chosen "to be holy and without blemish." Well, clearly, that doesn't describe me. But then, again, maybe it does describe me and us.

Mary, the mother of Jesus, was without blemish, and she was and is one of us, an example, maybe even a representative, and the Divine became human in her, one with the human race. Mary, one like me, is holy and without blemish, and in Jesus, the divine was united with the human race, in her, without blemish. And I am called to be like that, holy and without blemish. So in Christ, I am united to that, at least related to it. I am united to what is holy and without blemish. *We* are united with that.

Clearly, by myself, I am not "holy and without blemish,' but joined with Christ, I am somehow included in that. And Christ makes up for my weakness and my faults. He gives me strength to improve, to become a bit more "holy and without blemish." In him, I have redemption and *forgiveness.*

The key is my relationship, my union with Christ. The key is the union of the divine with the human in Christ, the God-Man, but is also my own union with Christ, for in Christ, I am an *adopted* son of God. I am more than I thought. I am better than I thought.

And Paul goes even further. The Father has made known to us the mystery of his will. He brought us into his confidence.

And in Christ, we were chosen for a purpose, united with Christ "in accord with the purpose of the One who accomplishes the intention of his will." I assume that means that we have work to do.

So how should I think about Christ.? I should think of myself as united with him as a friend, as a brother, sharing his values and work and his favor, sharing what we know of the mystery of his will, which God has made known to us.

Called to be, even if not yet there. And that's okay.

If Jesus Played Golf or Basketball

If Jesus played golf, what handicap would he have? If he played basketball, what would be his percentage of successful three-point shots?

Of course, this is unrealistically hypothetical, pure speculation. We know of no golf courses in first-century Israel. And archeologists have discovered no basketball hoops, to my knowledge. However, little kids play, and teenagers enjoy competitive games, so it is likely that Jesus did those. Golf and modern basketball? Probably not.

But what if? What do you think?

First golf as I know that better.

Jesus said, "Whoever has seen me has seen the Father" (John 14:9). Jesus is equal to the Father. God. All-powerful, Creator, all-everything. Therefore, would Jesus, the God-Man, have a low handicap in golf, better than the pros? (For nongolfers, a golf handicap is roughly the difference between what you score and par, and par is what you should score. It's a bit more complicated than that, but that's the gist of it. So if a player usually shoots 80, and par is 72, his handicap would be about 8. If the player shoots 82 that day, his or her net score would be 74.) A professional golfer's, or very good golfer's, handicap would probably be a plus handicap, say a plus 2, meaning they would generally score better than par. (A score of 70 would result in a net score of 72; par 70 "plus 2.")

One could argue that Jesus would be a zero handicap or a plus handicap. He would hit every shot perfectly, long and straight drives, shots to the green the right distance, and he would sink many putts. And in basketball, he would sink every three-point shot as well as every shorter jump shot. After all, he is God, God with us.

But I don't think that's a correct prediction. Saint Paul emphasized that Jesus became Man, true Man, like us. Philippians 2:5–8 reads:

> Though he was in the form of
> God, he did not regard equality
> with God something to be grasped.
> Rather, he emptied himself, tak-
> ing the form of a slave, coming in
> human likeness; and found human
> in appearance, he humbled him-

self, becoming obedient to death,
even death on a cross.

And the letter to the Hebrews (2:17–18) says, "Therefore, *he had to become like his brothers and sisters in every way*, that he might be a merciful and faithful high priest before God to expiate the sins of the people. Because he himself was tested through what he suffered, he is able to help those who are being tested" (emphasis added). He could understand and relate to us, relate to what we go through.

Like us in every way, obviously, except sin.

One person suggested that Jesus would have a golf handicap of 34 (that's high), so he could understand suffering and the need to improve. And besides, he had no time to practice, especially after he began his public ministry. On the other hand, before that, he had a job, he was a carpenter (Mark 6:3), so maybe he could have played golf sometimes.

Or maybe Jesus would have been a pretty good but nonprofessional golfer, like a 10 or 15 handicap player. Truly man like us, he would still be a pretty good player but not invoking his divine powers. That way, he'd be a good example, encouraging but not overwhelming, especially if he had a good attitude when he missed shots. More important, he would be understanding of those who are not particularly good at golf and often miss shots.

And carrying that over into real life, not this hypothetical, this "what if," the fact is that Jesus is understanding of faults and sins. He was and is empathetic. If his golf game had faults and weaknesses, in a nonmoral sense, wouldn't that have shown that he could understand others' moral faults and weaknesses, even those who were his own partners in (the game of) life?

I'd argue the very same way about three-point basketball shots. He'd probably be good but not perfect. And he'd be a good sport, a good winner, and not a sore loser. And his team would lose a few games and not be perfect.

Kind of like his Church.

What do you think?

Or maybe each golfer and each basketball player could think Jesus would be a player just like him or her, really good, really average, or just a beginner. But "like me."

Truly God and truly Man. Redeemer, Forgiver, Brother, Friend. Understanding.

Theotokos

Should Mary, the Mother of Jesus, be called (in Greek) *Christotokos*, rather than *Theotokos*, Christ-Bearer, rather than God-Bearer? *Theotokos* in Greek means the one who gave birth to God, usually translated in English as Mother of God.

Is that really important? Or is it some technicality discussed by scholars and high-level theologians? And is it a question about Mary? Or is it about Jesus? And does this affect me?

Around the year AD 431, it was considered very important. Christian Church leaders (and we were all one Church back then) came from all over to meet in Ephesus, in present-day Turkey, to discuss that. Ephesus was once a large and important city and important trading center in the Mediterranean region. Travel to there could not have been easy, certainly not an easy journey by cruise ship to a nearby port and a short bus ride like today. (Today, Ephesus is a tourist destination to archeological ruins, including to a home thought to have been that of the Virgin Mary.)

And more to the point, why was the issue that important? And how does it affect our own belief about Jesus?

What's the point?

Mary is the Mother of Jesus; therefore, the Mother of the Christ, the Messiah. "Hail Mary, full of grace, the Lord is with thee," we pray. But since Jesus as the Word of God preexisted his earthly birth, was it proper to call Mary the Mother of God? Or should she "only" be called the Mother of the Christ, *Christotokos*? Is it correct to pray, as we do, "Holy Mary, Mother of God, pray for us…"

The Church, through its leaders in formal Council in AD 431, concluded that Jesus was one person; one person with two natures, divine and human. He was not a dual person, not split, not a sort of conjunction. He was one person. He had two natures. His Godhead was fully united with his human nature in this one person. He fully joined the human race.

God. Jesus is equal to the Father. "Philip said, to him, Master, show us the Father and that will be enough for us. Jesus said to him… Whoever has seen me has seen the Father" (John 14:9). And, again, he said, "The Father and I are one" (John 10:30).

Man. Jesus is Man. In him the divine and the human were joined. His full human nature is necessary for our redemption as his divine nature joins with his human nature in one person, he became one of us, he joined us to heal us. This is, of course, important, and important for us. And this is another reminder and another teaching that our God is with us and calls us to share in his life and grace.

Jesus is the Christ, the Messiah, the Savior, Son of God, equal to the Father, who joined the human race, for the purpose of bringing the human race into proper relationship with the Godhead.

Mary's role was to give human birth to the person. She is Mother of Christ, *Christotokos*, and she is the one who carried the Godhead into the world, *Theotokos*. It is really a statement about Jesus, which affirms that the second person of the Trinity, who was born into history as fully human, is really "God with us."

So, this belief, formally stated in AD 431, which seems quite technical and esoteric, is actually extremely important for our faith today, our faith in Jesus, and emphasizes the amazing miracle of the God with us, the extreme event of the Almighty Godhead becoming one with the human race.

And it is important for us. A fifth-century theologian regarded the embodiment of God in the person of Jesus to be so mystically powerful that it spread out from the body of the God-Man, into the rest of the race, to reconstitute human nature into a graced and deified condition of the saints, one that promised immortality and transfiguration to believers (*Wikipedia*, Cyril of Alexandria).

So each of us is pretty special, closer to God than we may have thought.

He Was a Carpenter

"Where did this man get all this? ... Is he not the carpenter, the son of Mary?" (Mark 6:2–3).

Jesus was a man. He was a carpenter. That sounds pretty normal and pretty human. When he was twelve, he was found speaking impressively with teachers in the temple area (Luke 2:41–50). So, yes, he was special. But after that event, he went down to Nazareth and was obedient to Mary and Joseph, and from that time, he grew in wisdom, age, and favor before God and man (Luke 2:52). Again, that sounds like a very normal, human life.

We don't hear anymore until much later, when he began his public life.

The point is it seems to me that God entered *our* world, became one of us. And that's also where he calls us—in *our* world and in *our* lives, our normal lives, our regular lives, *our Monday through Friday, Saturday, lives.*

We are to be his followers on Mondays, not just on Sundays; in our regular lives, not just in church;

in our regular times, not just in our times of private or public prayer.

Sure, there are Sundays, church days, days of rest, days of reflection. In Mark's Gospel (6:31), at Jesus' invitation, the apostles went off to a deserted place to rest a while. People today often do that, go on retreat, go off to a special place to rest, to think. They spend a day or two or more in a special place to pray and think about what's really important, their work lives, their families, and neighborhoods. But that's the exception. Most days, they are in their regular lives, their families, and neighborhoods.

In fact, even when Jesus and the apostles went off in the boat and tried to be in a deserted place, people came from towns and villages, from their regular lives to hear him. And Jesus taught them. It was hard to find a special place and a special time to rest, to think, and to pray. We are where we are, not always where we wish we could be.

The letter to the Hebrews says, "Through him let us continually offer to God a sacrifice of praise, that is, the fruit of lips that confess his name." Then it continues, "Do not neglect to do good and to share what you have; God is pleased by sacrifices of that kind" (Hebrews 13:16). God is pleased by sacrifices of *that* kind.

The world needs priests, ministers, and religious people who teach, preach, sanctify, pray, heal, lead, people who know the Lord and know about the Lord. But the world also needs decent people, and more of them, who do regular work in the world. The world needs plumbers and electricians who fix, carpenters who build, parents who nurture and comfort, accountants and lawyers who organize, and government officials who serve, doctors and nurses who heal, people who clean, park cars, trim bushes, and cut grass.

The Lord and his grace are in the world, not apart from it. And his grace works within and through people, sometimes, even when they don't know, don't realize that it is God's grace at work through them. The days are coming, says the Lord, when all from the least to the greatest will know the Lord (see Jeremiah 31:31–34). Could that mean that people do good works, the Lord's work, even when they think they don't know him? Maybe their actions and good works show that they are doing the Lord's work, even if they don't realize they are. Maybe the Lord is working through them.

A man, one time, questioned whether he should leave his work, his successful business, and become a missionary. He decided, however, that it was better to stay where he was, be good at what he did, provide the service he was doing, be an example of a good, honest person, hardworking, continue to be a good husband and father where he was. Yes, he was active in the Church but also active in the community, in his world.

He was religious on Mondays as well as on Sundays. The book of Genesis says, "Fill the earth and subdue it… Have dominion" over the whole earth (Genesis 1:28). Build the earth where you are, in your regular lives.

The Incarnation means that God became Man, the divine and human are joined. The holy place on Sunday is joined with the so-called secular place on Monday. And the Holy Spirit in people on Sunday is the same Holy Spirit in the actions of decent people doing good things on Monday, religious things as well as so-called secular. The peaceful feeling on Sunday is related to the good effort on Monday. And Thursday. It is the Lord's work we are and should be doing both in church on Sunday and in the rest of our worlds, the rest of the week.

"The Word became flesh and made his dwelling among us" (John: 1:14).

About the Author

Dennis Sullivan has been a priest, lawyer, and utility executive and is a husband and father. He is currently retired and enjoys playing golf and traveling. He has been a lifelong-believing Catholic Christian.

www.ingramcontent.com/pod-product-compliance
Lightning Source LLC
Chambersburg PA
CBHW022029150726
47990CB00002B/887